500 MORE
ALL TIME FUNNIEST
GOLF JOKES,
STORIES,
& FAIRWAY WISDOM

500 MORE
ALL TIME FUNNIEST
GOLF JOKES,
STORIES,
& FAIRWAY WISDOM

Copyright © 1997 by Ron & Sheila Stewart

ISBN: 0-9656856-1-6

Published by

Acadia Scale Press

Books by Sheila & Ron Stewart

500 All Time Funniest Golf Jokes,
Stories & Fairway Wisdom

500 More All Time Funniest Golf Jokes,
Stories & Fairway Wisdom

Another 500 All Time Funniest Golf Jokes,
Stories & Fairway Wisdom

500 All Time Funniest *Slightly Off The Fairway*
Golf Jokes, Stories & Fairway Wisdom

500 All Time Funniest *Husband & Wife*
Golf Jokes, Stories & Fairway Wisdom

500 All Time Funniest *Almost On The Green*
Golf Jokes, Stories & Fairway Wisdom

500 All Time Funniest *All Over The Golf Course*
Golf Jokes, Stories & Fairway Wisdom

Dogs & Clouds & Love & Life

The Professor Murders

The Sandstorm Connection

For Craig and Steven.

5 0 0 MORE
ALL TIME FUNNIEST
GOLF JOKES,
STORIES,
& FAIRWAY WISDOM

"I've been working on a new swing," a golfer informed the others in his foursome, "and I'm really looking forward to trying it out." He then teed up his ball and sliced it into the side of a house beside the fairway.

"I'm not sure . . . ," one of the other golfers observed, "but I think I've seen you use that swing before."

"What's the rough like on this course?" one golfer asked another who was just about to take his first drive of the day.

"Don't know," the golfer on the tee replied. "I haven't hit my ball yet."

"I finally found the perfect golf swing," one golfer informed another.

"Let's see it," the other golfer replied.

"I can't show it to you just like that," the first golfer answered. "It only comes to me every twenty-five times or so."

"The problem with your ball landing in the rough," a golf instructor said to his students, "is that when you hit it, you sometimes get a flyer."

"What's a flyer?" a student asked.

"It's when your golf ball pops up in the air, takes off, and doesn't stop when it lands," the instructor informed him.

"That's the type of shot I've been looking for," the student replied.

"What would you say if I told you I had just purchased a new set of golf clubs," a husband informed his wife, "and the manufacturer guarantees that if I don't shoot par within five years, that they will give me my money back?"

"I would say they've pretty well sized up the quality of your game by the length of time they've given themselves to get out of town," his wife answered.

One of the most difficult aspects in the game of golf is pretending that we actually know how to play.

"How would you judge my golf game today?" a husband asked his wife. "Excellent . . . ? Very good . . . ? Good . . . ? Fair . . . ?"
"Poor . . . ?" he blurted in exasperation when she didn't answer. "Rotten . . . ?"
His wife thought for a moment, then said, "What comes after rotten?"

Funny thing about golf, if you want your ball to go 200 yards, you just take a nice smooth swing. If you want your ball to go only 150 yards, you whack the heck out of it.

"What's the difference between a happy golfer and a miserable golfer?"
"About 20 strokes."

"I would like to play golf somewhere that matches my skills," a golfer said. So they took him to a cow pasture on the edge of a swamp.

One golfer claimed to have hit a drive 300 yards. When asked if anyone had witnessed the drive, he had to admit they hadn't.

The next time he told the story, the drive was 325 yards.

"What should I do if my golf ball is in an unplayable lie?" a beginner asked an experienced golfer.

"Move your ball two club lengths, take a drop, and hit it from there," the experienced golfer responded.

A while later the two golfers met again.

"Well," the experienced golfer asked, "was your ball in a better lie when you took the two club lengths and a drop?"

"No," the beginner replied. "It was still in the lake."

"My husband and I played golf today with a man who wouldn't stop swearing."

"Were you offended?"

"Yes I was."

"What about your husband? Was he offended?"

"No. He thought the other golfer was just trying to strike up a conversation."

"Are you a good golfer?" a golfer was asked.
"I'm the second best golfer on this golf course," the golfer replied.
"Wow!" the questioner exclaimed, then asked, "Who's the best?"
"From what they tell me," the golfer answered, "they all are."

Most golfers do not have an inferiority complex, but they sure could use one.

A golfer went to a palm reader to see if she could help him straighten out his drives. She kept going off his hand.

I once tried night golf. I couldn't see my ball. My score was the same.

"I really didn't want to bring my wife golfing. She's slow, she can't hit the ball very far, she laughs at my game, and she nags the heck out of me."
"Then why did you bring her?"
"She's the only person who'll play with me."

"My husband got angry after a shot and broke his five iron," a wife said to a golf pro in the pro shop. "Would you have a replacement?"
"I'm sorry," the pro answered. "We don't carry husbands."

The very best golf games often contain things they are not supposed to contain, such as good conversation and a lot of laughter.

"I had a very close call with golf this morning," one wife said to another.
"Oh?" the other wife answered. "Did you almost get hit by a ball?"
"No," the first wife replied. "My husband almost asked me to go with him."

Other golfers are always asking me, "What did you get on that hole?" I think it makes them feel better when they add up their own scores.

"Why don't we skip the swing," a beginning golfer said to an instructor, "and go right to the difficult stuff."

"It says in this book that golfers are among the most intelligent and imaginative of all sports people," a golfer informed his wife.

"I believe it," she replied.

"Really?" he exclaimed.

"Of course," she said. "You'd have to be to make up all those stories."

Have you ever noticed that after a bad shot, golfers take another practice swing . . . like they're trying to duplicate it?

"My husband hit his golf ball over a row of houses three fairways ago, and I haven't seen him since."

"That's awful, that you haven't seen your husband for three fairways."

"I know. He's usually back by now."

Two golf instructors met after a clinic.

One said to the other, "Well, how are your new students doing?"

"Not bad," the second instructor answered. "They seem to have the cussing and complaining part down. Now if they could just golf . . . ."

I was describing my golf game to my wife, and she fell asleep. I was so upset that I decided to describe it to myself. I fell asleep.

"I consider myself to be better than the average player," a golfer announced to the club pro. "You realize that's not saying a lot," the pro answered.

"What is your husband doing today?"
"He's thinking about cleaning up the yard."
"Is that where he is? Out in the yard?"
"No. The golf course. That's where he does his thinking."

They say your golf game begins to deteriorate after age forty. My game usually begins to deteriorate right after someone says, you're teeing off in two minutes.

A golfer was asked what the difference was between shooting a low score and shooting a high score.
"Eye witnesses," he answered.

Another golfer said to me, "That was a bad lie you had for your last shot out of the rough."
I didn't even know he was listening.

We should never display arrogance or a condescending attitude when a fellow golfer hits a drive into a lake. Instead, we should offer comments that might encourage the other golfer, such as, "Good shot. Could you show me how you did that? Was your ball dirty? What club are you going to use for your next shot? I have a row boat at home if you need it . . . ."

"This essay describing your father's golf game is exactly the same as the stories handed in by three other students," a teacher said.
"I know," the student answered. "They were all in the same foursome."

"And now," a golfer said to the others in his foursome as he placed his ball on the tee, "I shall snatch victory from the jaws of defeat."
Unfortunately, the other golfers were laughing so hard that it distracted him, and his drive went into the lake again.

"I hope I never have to play golf again with that woman over there," a wife complained to her husband after completion of a game. "Imagine recording an eleven on a par three hole."

"Is that what she gave herself?" the husband asked, "an eleven?"

"No," the wife exclaimed, "that's what she gave me."

"My husband claims he made me the golfer I am today," one wife said to another as they searched along a lake for their first drives of the day. "I figured, what the heck, as long as he's willing to take the blame . . . ."

"When did you first suspect that your game was coming apart?" one golfer asked another.

"I'm not entirely sure," the other golfer replied, "but I think it might have been somewhere during the down swing on my first drive."

A senior citizen took up golf.

"Sometimes it takes many years to learn the game of golf," the golf pro advised.

"I'm in no hurry," the senior citizen answered.

First golfer: "I went into that yard over there to get my ball, and the home owner gave me two seconds to get off her property."
Second golfer: "She must be getting crankier. Yesterday she gave me five seconds."

One wife asked another what her husband did for entertainment.
"He golfs," the second wife replied.
"And what do you do for entertainment?" the first wife asked.
The second wife smiled. "I ask him how his game went."

"I reached the green with a drive, six pitches, and a throw."
"What's a throw?"
"It's what you use after you've missed six pitches."

One of the longest periods in a golfer's life: The time it takes a perfectly placed shot to roll from the center of the green, to the edge of the green, then off the green, and into the lake beside the green.

"I noticed that your husband isn't swearing in his golf game today."

"That's because I helped him get it out of his system before we came."

"How did you do that?"

"I had him instal a new faucet in the kitchen sink."

Two genies were watching a duffer as he thrashed around in the rough.

"I appeared before him last night and said that I would give him any wish he wanted," the first genie reported.

"And what did he wish for?" the second genie asked.

"He said he wanted to be a golfer."

"And did you give him his wish?"

"Yes I did."

"So why is he still in the rough?"

"He didn't say he wanted to be a good golfer."

"I have some good news and some bad news for you," one golfer said to another. "The good news is, you made it over the lake in front of the green. The bad news is, you also made it over the lake behind the green."

"How would you describe the round of golf you just shot?" a golfer was asked after completing a poor round.

"It deserves to be shot," he replied.

"Your golf ball just hit my house," a homeowner complained to a golfer.

"I'm terribly sorry," she answered. "I was told that it would help my accuracy if I picked out a house behind the green and aimed for it."

"Well, at least you hit your ball straight," the homeowner said.

"I'm afraid not," she replied. "I was aiming for that house over there."

My husband likes to talk to his golf ball. Many times, when he's in the rough, I have heard him tell it where he wants it to go. I have also heard him tell his drives and his putts where to go. Once, I even heard him tell the entire golf course where to go.

Golf is a thinking man's game. Of course, if you spend too much time thinking, you might miss the enjoyment.

Happy golfers are happy people, and vice versa.

"I know 286 different ways to hit a golf ball."
"How do you remember them all?"
"I don't. They just come to me during my swing."

"What was your final score?" a husband asked.
"I believe ninety-seven," his wife replied.
"Aren't you sure?" he said.
"Well . . . ," she responded hesitantly.
"How many times did you add it up?"
"Four."
"It must be ninety-seven then," the husband exclaimed. "If you added it up four times."
"Wait," the wife interrupted.
"What?"
"Don't you want to know what I got the other three times?"

"Somewhere in this world," a golfer moaned as another golf ball sailed into the rough, "there must be a golf club that I can hit a fairway with."
"I'm sorry," his playing partner replied, "but I'm using my putter."

Golf is one of those feel better sports. No matter how bad you play, you can always find someone who plays worse. It makes you feel better.

Golf Pro: "Can I see your swing?"
Golfer: "Certainly. Which one?"

A newspaper reporter was interviewing the manager of a golf course.
"How many golfers do you have, broken down by their scores?" he asked.
"All of them," the manager responded.

"I'm a little concerned for the safety of our neighbors," one wife said to another. "My husband has put up a net against the side of the house, and he's practicing hitting golf balls."
"Is he missing the net?"
"He's missing the house."

The problem with shooting a good round of golf is that it ends too soon. The problem with shooting a poor round of golf is that it doesn't end soon enough.

Joe's first went into a sand trap. His second went into a lake. His third went into another sand trap. Joe never could putt.

They say that in the game of golf, you learn from your mistakes. I sure must have learned a lot.

We really don't hear golfers swear all that much. What we do hear is a lot of muttering. Of course, in that muttering there could be a considerable amount of swearing.

"What club do you think you're going to need for that shot?" one golfer asked another who was heading into the rough after his ball.
"About a nine iron," the golfer said.
"You'll never get your ball to the green with a nine iron," the first golfer exclaimed.
"I'm not trying to get it to the green," the second golfer said as he continued his walk. "I'm trying to get it back to the fairway."

Every once in a while we need to remind ourselves that golf is just a game.

"My husband has added 25 yards to his drives."
"Really? What did he change?"
"The way he describes his drives."

"What did you get on that hole?" one golfer asked another.
"I think I shot a four," the second golfer said.
"I'd better give you a five, just to be sure," the golfer who had asked the question replied.
"In that case," the other golfer responded, "I think I shot a three."

"I don't get much pleasure out of golf," one business executive said to another. "I just come out here with other business people because it's part of my job."
"But I saw you out here on Saturday."
"Oh yeah, well, then it was pleasure."

On a 525 yard par five hole, two golfers topped their first drives which traveled only twenty-five yards from the tee. As they approached their golf balls to take their second shots, one was heard to say to the other, "I think you're away, so you go first."

Two married couples were playing in a foursome. One husband and wife watched as the other husband helped his wife with her club selection, her ball location on the tee, her set up, her swing, her foot alignment, and anything else he could think of, after which she drove her ball into a lake.

As the two husbands frowned at the errant shot, the other wife commented, "I think he should take at least some of the blame. He showed her how to put it there."

"What are you reading?" one wife asked another. "My New Year's resolution," the other answered. After reading it herself, the first wife said, "What on earth would possess you to write a resolution that says you won't complain about your husband going golfing?" "Oh, I didn't write it," the second wife replied. "He did."

"My drives are getting much better." "What do you mean, better? Your golf balls are still going into the lake." "True, but if you've noticed, they're landing closer to shore."

If you take a really good look at a golfer and a golf course, you have to wonder which is playing which.

The law of averages says that after so many bad shots, we're bound to hit a good shot. The law of averages doesn't always apply in golf.

Two retired men were discussing their wives' golfing skills.
"Fortunately," one of them said, "the most critical aspect of my wifes's game has never changed, so her score has remained the same."
"What aspect is that?" the other asked.
"Filling out her score card."

A golf pro was watching a student who was not doing very well in a practice session. Her swings were slicing, hooking, catching only part of the ball, and sometimes even missing the ball completely.
After a moment the golf pro asked, "Which club are you using?"
With an optimistic smile she looked up and said, "Do you think it could be the club . . . ????"

"Does your husband golf?"
"He makes a living at it."
"Oh, he's a professional."
"No, a grounds keeper."

Everything I need to know about golf, I learned from my brother.
I learned that it's only a game.
I learned not to get upset about a poor shot, and to get excited about a good shot, whether it's mine or someone elses.
I learned that the people I play with are much more important than the game itself.
I learned that the rules aren't all that important, as long as we all play by the same rules.
I learned to respect other golfers, and the golf course.
I learned that the enjoyment we receive is much more important than the score we shoot.
I learned that I really like playing golf with my brother.

"Is it difficult to learn a new golf swing?" a young man asked an old timer.
"Not at all," the old timer replied. "I learn a new one every time I play."

"It was the strangest thing," a husband said. "There I was, dreaming about being on the golf course, and when I woke up I was on the first tee."

His wife believed everything he said, having had a similar experience. "Same thing happened to me," she said. "There I was, dreaming I had gone shopping, and when I woke up, I was wearing a diamond necklace."

It was the last time the husband had that dream.

1st bystander: "Why are those four golfers huddled together in the middle of the fairway?"

2nd bystander: "One of their golf balls landed there, and they're trying to figure out who it belongs to."

A husband left his golf clubs leaning against the trunk of the car while he went into the house to answer the telephone. By the time he came out he had forgotten he left them there. Not thinking, he got into the car, started it up, and backed over them.

Later as his wife and a neighbor examined the mangled clubs, his wife explained. "My husband did that to them after his last golf game."

"How bad were playing conditions on that golf course, you ask. They weren't too bad . . . once they finished scything the fairways."

Two duffers are playing a round of golf. One says to the other, "What did you get on that last hole?"
"I shot a twelve," the second duffer answers.
"Always bragging," the first duffer replies.

"My husband does so have a lot of good golf shots," one wife said to another. "He just hasn't found the need to use any of them yet."

A golfer, who was having a bad game and getting a little desperate, prayed, "God, please let me hit just one fairway today."
After he took his shot, another golfer exclaimed, "You did, you did hit a fairway. Now, stay right there while I go see which one."

You know you're in for a tough round of golf when your first drive and your first divot both go the same distance.

"I can tell the quality of shot my husband makes by the amount of swearing he does. For instance, when he hits a really awful shot he does a lot of swearing, when he hits just a poor shot he does a little swearing, and when he hits a reasonably good shot he doesn't swear at all."

"And what does he do when he hits an excellent shot?"

"For some reason he goes back to swearing."

Two golfers were in the rough, searching for their wayward drives.

"Is this one yours?" one of them asked, pointing toward a ball.

The other golfer broke into a broad smile as she examined the ball. "Why, yes it is, thank you very much," she exclaimed, then added, "Now, could you also help me find the one I lost today."

"Why does your husband act so strange and do so many funny things when he golfs?" a wife was asked.

"I think it's because he has spent so much of his life in a dysfunctional environment," she replied.

"His family . . . ?"

"His foursome."

Have you ever wondered what the force is that turns the sky from sunny to rain during the walk from the club house to the first tee.

"Yesterday I hit a golf ball so far I lost it."
"I do that all the time."
"Really? When?"
"Whenever I manage to hit it."

"They tell me that we should always plan ahead in golf, so that after we hit our first shot we will be in a good position to hit our second shot."
"Is that what you do?"
"Yes."
"And does it work?"
"Not usually."
"Why not?"
"My plan and my ball don't go to the same place."

"I'm not going to take golf lessons any more," one wife said to another. "I don't see why I should have to pay a golf instructor to tell me everything I'm doing wrong, when my husband does it for nothing."

A young woman who had taken up golf was having a discussion with a friend.

"Each time I meet an eligible bachelor," she said, "I have to ask myself, is this the man I want to spend every Saturday morning with for the rest of my life."

"I worry that no matter how many hours I practice, I will never get my golf score down into the seventies."

"Oh? And what is your score now?"

"112."

A husband was giving his wife encouragement on her first day of golf.

"That was a very good drive," he said as her shot missed the green by a hundred feet and landed in a lake. "Try another."

"That was also a good shot," he said as her second shot missed the green by the same amount and landed in the same lake. "Try another."

After informing his wife that her third shot into the lake was also a good shot and to try another, one of the other golfers in the foursome whispered, "I wonder if he knows what she's supposed to be aiming at."

"Are you sure this is your correct score?" a husband said suspiciously to his wife as he examined her score card at the completion of their game.

"You didn't happen to take a mulligan or two, or maybe a few, did you?" he asked, raising an eyebrow.

"You were in the rough beside that last fairway for quite a while," he said. "I don't suppose you might have perhaps taken a couple extra swings, or moved your ball to get a better lie . . . ?" He paused a moment. "Or accidentally gave it a little kick . . . ?"

"What about that hole where you hit your ball into the lake?" he pressed. "You know there are actually some golfers who refuse to give themselves a penalty stroke when they do something like that."

"And sometimes golfers forget to add a stroke here and there on their score cards," he said as he continued to examine the card. "You didn't inadvertently forget to add a few strokes, did you?"

Later, when his wife was talking to a friend, she was asked, "Did you learn a lot about golf from your husband today?"

"No," she replied, "but I think I might have discovered some new ways to lower my score."

"There's nothing I like better than a good golf game that lasts all day Saturday," one wife said to another.
"Oh, do you golf?"
"No. But my husband does."

A community college offered a course on how to reduce your golf score. The first lesson was dedicated to filling out the score card.

A husband noticed that on his wife's score card were some holes that she had marked with a zero.
"Why?" he asked.
"I prefer not to think about them," she replied.

"Nothing but narrow fairways, water, trees, rough, and sand traps," complained a golfer. "This sure is a challenging course."
"I know," the golf pro answered. "That's why they put it here."

Some of the happiest golfers play with wives. They send their husbands to work and then they go golfing.

A golfer was staring at a golf ball that was buried in deep rough. She was trying to figure out how she was going to get it out, when another golfer approached.

"I'm sorry," the other golfer said, "but that's my ball you were about to hit."

The first golfer took another look at the ball, smiled a broad smile, and replied, "Well, that's the best news I've heard all day."

There isn't all that much difference between professional golfers and the rest of us. Professionals hit the ball the same way we do. A little farther and straighter maybe . . . .

My husband isn't speaking to me, all because I congratulated him on making a good shot.

I didn't say anything when he drove his first ball into the lake, I didn't say anything when he lost his second ball in the rough, I still didn't say anything when he took seven shots to get his ball out of a sand trap. Even when his ball went back into the lake, I didn't say anything.

It wasn't until he kicked his ball and it landed a foot from the pin, and I said, "Hey, good shot." That's when he stopped talking to me.

Dear Golf Advisor: "I am a young woman who has begun golfing with my boyfriend. Although he is a very good golfer, so far he has not shown any interest in my game and refuses to help me with my swing. Can you offer any suggestions that will get him to help me correct my swing?"
Dear young woman golfer: "Yes. Marry him."

Dear golf advisor: "I am a young woman who golfs with three other women. Although I am having a thoroughly enjoyable time, I feel that I could learn more if I golfed with men who are more competitive."
Dear young woman golfer: "I too feel you could learn more if you golfed with men who are more competitive. The only thing you would not learn, is how to have a thoroughly enjoyable time."

If we really think about it, what we're trying to do is hit a golf ball the size of a small rock, with a club head the size of two small rocks, that is on the end of a four foot shaft, that is being swung at a hundred and some miles per hour, by a golfer who performs the function one day a week or twice a month. Is there any wonder we have difficulty hitting it straight.

A beginner's first shot went into a lake. His second shot went deep into the rough. His third shot crashed through the window of a nearby house. His fourth shot missed the course completely and bounced off a highway in the distance.

"New to the game?" another golfer asked.

The beginner looked surprised and said, "How could you tell that, after just four shots?"

"I shot eighty today," one golfer said to another.

"Really," the other golfer answered. "And which hole did you shoot it on?"

"My golf score this morning was the same as my husband's."

"Don't worry about it. The most important thing is that you're having fun."

"I hit four shots in a row into that lake and you don't even seem to be interested," a wife complained.

"I am interested," her husband replied. "I'm just more interested in seeing how many of them you put on your score card."

THE PUTT

He lined the ball up with his eye,
A simple putt to make,
One easy stroke into the cup,
Was all that it would take.

With confidence his putter moved,
The ball rolled straight and true,
It glided o'er the grassy green,
As to the hole it flew.

He knew not how it missed the cup,
Perhaps a blade of grass,
Had caused the ball to change its course,
And go on speeding past.

His second putt was lined up now,
Toward the cup it rolled,
He saw it take a solid line,
He knew he had it holed.

It must have been a gust of wind,
Or mark from someone's shoe,
Or dip or break or someone coughed,
That sent the ball askew.

He watched his third putt long and hard,
He studied all the breaks,
He squeezed his putter tight until
His hands began to ache.

The ball broke left, then right, then left,
Then ringed the orifice,
It didn't matter anymore,
He knew the putt would miss.

His fourth putt didn't take as long,
No worry or mistake,
He drove the golf ball off the green,
Into a distant lake.

****

A golfer was hit by a golf ball. As he lapsed into a coma, his wife sobbed, "And he was so proud of himself today. He finally shot a round of eighty."
Six months later when the golfer woke up, his first words were, "It was a seventy-nine."

I have to tell you, I'm getting just a little tired of other golfers saying to me, "Excuse me, but that's my ball. Your ball is back there."

Wife to husband: "I'm having trouble getting to sleep. Could you tell me about your golf game again?"

Four golfers were huddled together beside the fifteenth tee. A blanket of rain was pouring down on them, a biting wind was blowing into their faces, and they were soaked to the skin. As they strained to see through the wall of water that obliterated the fairway, one of them commented, "I sure feel sorry for the poor people who have to work today."

The golf course where I play is owned by an international conglomerate. My clubs came from Japan. My golf balls were made in Germany. My bag was assembled in Mexico. My glove was made in Taiwan. It's amazing how I can make so many countries rich with a game I can't afford and don't know how to play.

"Lately, I feel my golf game has really grown," one golfer said to another.
"Maybe it's because it spends so much time in water," the other golfer replied.

Disappointment is when someone beats you in a game of golf. Dejection is when they shoot 115, and beat you.

"My husband just bought a brand new, uniquely designed, guaranteed to eliminate his slice and add 25 yards to his drives, golf club."
"Could I see it?"
"Sure. It's out in the garage with his other ten or so, brand new, uniquely designed, guaranteed to eliminate his slice and add 25 yards to his drives, golf clubs."

"I don't think my new boyfriend is interested in marriage," one young woman said to another.
"How do you know?" the other asked.
"Because we went golfing together," the first replied, "and he didn't tell me how to hit even one shot."

"Where did you learn about golf?"
"Watching TV."
"What did you learn?"
"I learned that I'd rather be playing it than watching it."

"I couldn't decide whether to use a hard seven iron or a soft six iron to reach the green on that last hole."

"What did you use?"

"A hard seven iron, a soft six iron, two nine irons, three pitching wedges, and a chipper."

"I don't know if I should use a hard five iron or a hard four iron for this shot," one golfer said to another.

"Don't you mean a hard five iron, or a *soft* four iron?" the other golfer asked.

"No," the first golfer replied. "I mean a hard five iron or a hard four iron. No matter which club I use, it's going to be a hard shot."

A golfer was searching for a lost ball.

"What kind is it?" another golfer who had stopped to help asked.

Sheepishly, the golfer who had lost her ball replied, "I was worried that my drive might go into the lake, so I used a range ball. It's yellow, with a blue stripe around it."

"One good thing," the other golfer replied, "I don't think we'll have to worry about someone else hitting it by mistake."

I like to walk when we go golfing. My wife likes to ride. She figures if God had intended for us to walk she wouldn't have given us all those golf carts.

Two society women were comparing their golf games.
"My husband saved money by teaching me how to play," one said.
"My husband tried to do the same thing," the other answered, "but it cost him fourteen million dollars."
"How did that happen?" asked the first.
"I divorced the cheapskate," the other replied.

Our third or fourth time golfing is always easier than our first or second time. By the third or fourth time we've *accepted* that our game stinks.

"How was your golf game today?" a wife asked her husband.
"Do you want me to describe it, with or without cussing?" he answered.
"Without," she said.
"Then I have nothing to say," he replied.

I think I'll stop letting my wife look after our score card . . . .

I glanced at the card and said, "I think you forgot a couple strokes on your score."

She said, "No, I didn't."

I said, "Where are they then?"

She said, "I put them on your score."

"Ever since you gave me this swing," a golfer complained to a golf pro, "all my drives have been missing fifty yards to the right."

"So, come back tomorrow," the golf pro replied, "and I'll give you another swing."

"I stopped golfing. Golf courses remind me too much of gambling casinos."

"How so?"

"No windows, no clocks . . . ."

"Have you noticed how having a good lie can reduce a golf score by several strokes?"

"You mean, like my ball landing in the fairway instead of the rough?"

"No. I mean later on in the clubhouse, when you're describing your game."

"How was your husband's golf game today?"
"Not very good. But give him a few hours. It'll improve."

A cocky young man was applying for a job as golf instructor. One of the questions he was asked was, "What would you do if you were lying six shots on a par five?"
"Don't know," he answered.
"Why not?" he was asked.
"Never had to," he replied.

A good golfer is one who has convinced others that he's the best. A great golfer is one who has convinced himself that he's the best.

Golfers like almost everything about the game, except the group ahead and the group behind, and the other golfers who make up their foursome, and players who are too slow or too fast, and the clerk who hands out the tee times, and the weather, and the course conditions, and the location of the pin, and their drives, and their putts, and their equipment, and their score, and their . . . .

A wife decided to subscribe to a local newspaper, ordering only the Saturday and Sunday editions. Her husband was perturbed.

"There is nothing in those newspapers," he complained, "just store advertising and news articles they've been saving. There is no real news and no real value. I'd gladly give up the weekend newspapers for Thursday's."

"What value does Thursday's newspaper have that the weekend newspapers don't have?" his wife asked.

"Golf coupons," he replied.

After driving four golf balls into a lake, a golfer hurled his one wood straight down the fairway. It was the first time anything from his golf bag had ever landed there.

"Is this a par five hole?" a golfer asked as he prepared to fill in his score card.

"No," another golfer answered. "It's a par four hole."

The first golfer looked back down the fairway, mentally counted the strokes he had taken, added his putts with his fingers, entered his score, smiled to himself, and said, "Close enough."

"You're still slicing," a golf instructor said to a student, "but that doesn't bother me."
"If you had to go find them like I do, it would sure bother you," the student replied.

"I couldn't shoot my own age in golf, so I decided to see if I could shoot my father's age."
"Oh? How old is your father?"
"Yesterday, he would have been 109."

"Every once in a while, you should take some more lessons," a golf pro informed his student, "because sooner or later you will forget a portion of what you have learned."
"Good idea," the student agreed. "I'm sure I will eventually forget some of what I have learned about my swing, my putting, my chipping and pitching, and then there is my slice."
"Oh no," the golf pro replied, "you will never forget your slice."

A wife was sorting her golf balls.
"Good balls and range balls?" her husband asked.
"Straight balls and crooked balls," she replied.

If you want a teenager to get a hole in one, just say, "Whatever you do, don't hit your first shot into that little hole down there."

"I can always tell when my husband hits a good golf shot by the look that comes over his face as he watches where his ball lands."
"Excitement?"
"Surprise."

Wife: "Honey, I think I might have gotten your golf clubs wet."
Husband: "How could you possibly get my golf clubs wet?"
Wife: "I accidentally dropped them in the lake."
Husband: "How could you drop them in the lake? They were on the back of the golf cart."
Wife: "That's the other thing I wanted to talk to you about."

"Another golf brochure!" a husband complained. "Where do all these golf equipment companies get my name?"
"I don't know," his wife replied. "Unless it's from all the checks you keep sending them."

After his wife had given him the number of strokes she had taken on a hole, a husband remarked, "Are you sure you've forgotten enough of them?"

One golfer is so cheap . . . . His golf clubs are used, his golf balls are used, his tees are used. Even the golf course he plays on has been used.

My husband is an insomniac golfer. He won't let me fall asleep while he's describing his game.

I once asked the clerk in a golf shop for a price on some golf balls. He told me they were $69.00 each. I asked him why so much? He said their manager used to work in a hospital.

The three toughest shots in a golfer's game: The ones that take him from an 85 to a 72.

"What's the difference between a hook and a slice?"
"About three hundred feet."

A wife was asked why she enjoyed her golf game so much more than her husband enjoyed his.

"Because I shot a low score and he shot a high score," she answered.

"What does he consider to be a high score?" she was asked.

"78."

"And what do you consider to be a low score?"

"97."

My husband is always thinking ahead of his next drive, about fifty yards ahead.

A golfer in our foursome has a very short attention span. Every time he hits nine or ten golf balls into a lake, he quits.

"What is golf?" a young boy asked his mother.

"Mostly, it's a game where men sit around and tell each other how good they are," his mother answered.

"Do they ever talk about how bad they are?" the boy asked.

"No," his mother replied. "When that's happening they usually don't talk at all."

I saw a driver advertised that will cure my slice, correct my hook, and solve any other mistakes I should ever make in my game . . . . I asked myself, "What does it need me for?"

"Finally, I corrected my swing so that I'm hitting every ball the same."
"So, at last they're going straight . . . ?"
"No, but at least now I know which area of the lake to search."

One husband told his wife that he couldn't take her golfing with him because he barely had enough time to get in eighteen holes, let alone thirty-six.

I happen to like the mulligan. It saves me taking a lot of lessons.

First wife: "My husband says they're going to pay someone to caddie for them today in their golf game."
Second wife: "Amazing! Next thing you know, they'll be hiring someone to carry their clubs."

My husband's recollections of his golf games are usually a lot better than the games themselves. I can tell he has had a really poor game when even his recollections are bad.

"I'm not too sure about my new golf instructor. I was hitting a lot of golf balls into the rough, and he said he could help me. I told him all I wanted was to be able to hit my drives straight."
"So what happened?"
"My drives still went into the rough."
"And what did your new golf instructor have to say?"
"He said, they looked straight to me."

Golf is great for people who want to lose weight. After you pay for your tee time you can't afford to buy food.

A golfer was not having a very good day and had just missed another green by many yards.
"How far did your ball land from the hole?" another golfer asked, not seeing where his drive had gone.
"Which hole?" he replied.

"When did you quit golfing and become a grounds keeper?" a surprised golfer said to a man he had played several rounds with, who was now mowing grass on the edge of the fairway.

"Right after they told me they'd fire me if I didn't," the grounds keeper replied.

"How come there are nine or eighteen holes in golf instead of ten or twenty?"

"It was invented before the metric system."

For years I took lessons in an endeavor to improve my game. Then one day I played with a young golfer who had a perfect swing, the longest distance I had ever seen, and hit every ball straight down the middle of the fairway.

"Would you mind telling me where you took lessons?" I asked.

"I've never had a lesson," he said nonchalantly.

A visitor, admiring a set of golf clubs, asked a golfer, "Have you ever considered getting rid of them?"

"Yes," the golfer answered. "After just about every shot."

"My husband never learned how to golf," one wife confided to another.

"So," the other wife said, "lots of men haven't learned how to golf. Not everyone feels the need to play golf."

"But my husband golfs almost every week," the first wife replied.

An old timer and a duffer were talking golf. The old timer was describing the various swings he used for drives, shots from the fairway, getting out of the rough, hitting out of sand traps, pitching and chipping to the green, and other creative shots the duffer had never heard of.

"All in all," the old timer said with an air of confidence, "I probably use ten or twelve different types of swings, depending on where I am on the golf course."

"Heck," the duffer replied just a confidently, "I use more swings than that just to get off the tee box."

A salesman showed up at a golf course, selling an electronic counting device. He said it would help the golfers keep track of how many strokes they had taken on each hole. He never sold a one.

A Florida golfer and an Arizona golfer were comparing golf courses.

"We have a lot of ducks on our course," the Arizona golfer said, "and they can be a real nuisance at times. Do you have many ducks on your course?"

"No," the Florida golfer replied. "Nothing like ducks. All we have are alligators."

"I really envy the way you play golf," a beginner said to a golfer.

"Why thank you," the golfer replied.

The beginner continued, "I mean, to be able to play as bad as you do, and not get upset about it."

"How many fairways did you hit today?" one golfer asked another.

"I hit them all," the other golfer replied, "eventually . . . ."

A wife was asked why she constantly put up with her husband telling her how to hit the ball.

"It doesn't bother me," she answered, "and besides, every once in a while, he's right."

A beginner, who was still learning the game, asked the other golfers, "If my first drive hits a tree and bounces back onto the tee box, do I have to take a stroke or is it O.K. if I just start over?"

"I only took four mulligans today," a wife informed her husband after returning from a golf outing.

"I suppose four mulligans over eighteen holes isn't bad," her husband replied.

"No, no," the wife said. "That would be cheating. We're only allowed mulligans on the first hole."

"With all the different swings I have," a golfer who was having a bad day complained, "you would think at least one of them could hit a fairway."

"Do you think you would continue to golf after your wife died?" one husband asked another as their wives prepared to tee off.

"I really haven't given it much thought," the other husband replied. "I suppose it would depend on which hole she died."

A duffer, who was feeling particularly aggressive, said to the others in his foursome, "Today I finally become a golfer." And with that he sliced his very first drive into a lake.

After watching the golf ball disappear, another golfer responded, "Yep, you're a golfer all right."

Go figure. When we were teenagers, we couldn't hit a front lawn with a newspaper from five feet, and now we're surprised when we can't hit a golf green from two hundred yards.

One wife complained, "I wish my husband were half as conscientious about adding up his own score as he is about adding up my score."

A golfer went to the club pro for advice. "Something is wrong with my game," he said. "My first shot landed in a bird's nest in a tree, my second shot went down a rodent's hole, my third shot hit a duck four fairways over. My fourth shot landed in a flower pot on somebody's patio. What do you think could be wrong?" "I don't know," the pro answered, "but it sure isn't your eyesight."

"That's the fifteenth green I've hit today," one golfer said to another.

"I know what you mean," the other golfer replied. "I've been having the same problem with houses."

"Real golfers don't mind the rain," a golfer said as he scanned the water drenched course from a bar stool in the club house.

"I'm in mourning because of the death of my husband," one wife said to another.

"Oh, I'm very sorry to hear that," the other wife sympathized. "How did it occur?"

"Golf. He knows he should only play eighteen holes at one time, but he insisted on playing thirty-six."

"How long ago did he die?"

"Oh he hasn't yet, but he will, as soon as he gets home."

Two husbands are searching for their golf balls. One says to the other, "Why is it, you're supposed to be teaching your wife how to play, and she's in the fairway and you're in the lake?"

"Whenever I get a premonition that my golf ball is going into the rough, that's where it goes."
"And what happens if you have a premonition that your golf ball is going to hit the fairway?"
"I've never had that premonition."

A golfer bought a beautiful home overlooking the golf course, where he used to be able to afford to play golf, before he bought the home.

The owners of a golf course had just taken money from a businessman for a tee time.
"He claims it and we don't," one of them said.
"It all balances out."

The main difference between a good golf shot in a professional's game and a good golf shot in an amateur's game: A lot of skill with a little luck, and a little skill with a lot of luck.

"I think I've been spending a little too much time in the rough."
"What makes you say that?"
"One of my golf balls has grass growing on it."

I used to wonder how professional golfers could calculate their score cards without making a mistake. Then I figured it out. They don't have nearly as many strokes to add.

One of the golf instruction books promised to lower my score by at least five strokes. Another promised seven strokes. A third promised ten strokes. Still another promised twelve strokes. I bought them all. I figured I could use the thirty-four strokes.

A golfer visited a psychic and was told he would have the lowest score of everyone he'd be playing against in his game that weekend. Feeling rather confident, he took several bets that he would win. After playing the worst game of his life and shooting 118, he went back to the psychic and complained.

"I don't understand how I could have made a mistake like that," the psychic said. She pulled out her calendar for the day the golfer had visited, examined it, and then exclaimed, "Now I see what happened, you're the golfer. Somehow I got you confused with the customer who came in before you, the bowler."

"I enjoy golfing more when my wife tells me what to do."

"Really? What does she tell you to do?"

"She tells me to clean up the yard."

"Is golf an easy game to learn?" a beginner asked an old timer.

"Sometimes it's really easy, and sometimes it's really difficult," the old timer answered.

"I see a lot of golfers hitting their golf balls into the rough," the beginner said. "I suppose that's the difficult part."

"On the contrary," the old timer replied. "That's the easy part."

If you really want to succeed, you should enjoy what you're doing. Sometimes this applies to golf, sometimes it doesn't.

A lawyer was reading the last will and testament of a golfer. He went through the usual bequests, then added, "And to my golf pro, who kept telling me that my crappy golf game was worth much more than the thousands of dollars he charged me for lessons, I leave my golf game."

"When would you say you have met your goal, and when would you say you have exceeded your goal?" a golfer was asked.

After some thought, he answered, "I would say I have exceeded my goal when I find my ball in the fairway."

"Oh? Then when would you say you have met your goal?"

"When I find my ball."

A group of retired women had been discussing the possibility of shooting their age in golf.

"I gave up any hope of shooting my age long ago," one of them said, "so I've decided to see if I can shoot my weight."

"How are you doing?" one of the other women asked.

"I don't think I'm going to make it," the first woman replied, "unless I manage to gain a few pounds."

A wife asked her husband, who was looking after their score card, what her score was.

"A hundred," he answered.

"It can't be," she replied. "I don't usually reach a hundred until the fourteenth hole."

"What was your score in your golf game this morning?" one husband asked another.

"I was heading for a 95," the second husband said, "until my wife suggested an adjustment in my game that lowered my score by at least 10 strokes."

"Wow!" the first husband exclaimed. "What did she suggest?"

"She suggested I come home after the sixteenth hole," the second husband replied.

"Today," bragged a golfer, "we separate the golfers from the non golfers."

"Oh," another golfer responded. "And which group will you be in?"

Some golfers sure could use a tranquilizer when they play golf. Of course to most of us, golf is the tranquilizer.

A golfer was retrieving his ball from a lake when he fell in. As he floundered in the water, another member of his foursome walked by.

"Gaul dang it Jim," he said. "Did you come here to golf or to swim?"

Golfers would make great explorers. They know where they want to go, they just don't know which route they'll be taking.

"Isn't that man concerned about getting a sunburn, golfing without a hat?"
"Not where he does his best golfing."
"Where is that?"
"The bar in the club house."

I purchased some new golf balls made out of space age materials. Every time I hit one, it goes somewhere I've never been before.

What I don't understand is, how can the most beautiful drive I ever saw, go one hundred yards straight down the middle of the fairway, and then suddenly make a right turn.

"How is your husband's golf game coming?"
"Really good. He was in a tournament yesterday, and would have won except for one thing."
"What was that?"
"Some other golfers showed up."

"Where did you get the brown and green golf shoes?" one golfer asked another.

"Oh shut up," the first golfer snapped.

"What's wrong with him?" the second golfer said, turning to the first golfer's wife.

"His shoes were white when he started today," she replied.

Golfers do not make fools of themselves. The game does that. But they certainly are willing accomplices.

I finally relented and let a friend borrow my golf clubs. "Please treat them the way you would if they were your own," I said. He threw one into a lake, wrapped one around a tree, bent two others, and lost three. It was my own fault. I should have asked him how he treated his own.

A dedicated golfer never quits. Throw his one wood into a lake, maybe. Bend his five iron in three places, possibly. Swear for four and a half hours, certainly. Walk off the course in disgust and vow never to return, every weekend. But quit, never.

A golfer drove his golf ball into a gravel pit that ran along the edge of a golf course.

"Heck of a sand trap," he exclaimed as he hit his ball and continued with his game.

"I agree with you," one golfer said to another after watching a shot. "I also would have been positive that your ball hit the green, if I hadn't seen the splash."

"We're having a thirty-three percent off, water damage sale," a clerk informed some golfers.

"On golf equipment?"

"No, the course. The last six holes are flooded."

Wives are lucky. They only have to play one golf game. A husband has to play two golf games, his own and his wife's.

First golfer: "I don't understand why your wife is so happy? She just shot 110, which is a ridiculously high score."

Second golfer: "I know, but it's the lowest ridiculously high score she's ever had."

"The golfers ahead of us were so slow, I thought I would fall asleep."
"What kept you awake?"
"The golfers behind us."

"Is your husband an angry golfer?"
"I don't know."
"Why don't you know?"
"He hasn't talked since he took up the game."

I remember my first golf game like it was this morning, slicing balls into the rough, hooking them into the water, taking eight putts to sink a ball. Come to think about it, my first golf game really was like the game I played this morning.

A golfer was just about to tee up his ball to begin play on the back nine when a friend ran up to him.
"Jim," the friend said, "I just went by your place to see if you were there. I looked in the window and saw a man making love to your wife."
Jim thought for a moment, then stepped up to his ball. "Let's see if we can hurry this game up a little," he said. "I have to be getting home."

"Our foursome was tied with another foursome at the end of the tournament," a golfer informed his wife, "and the other golfers said they wanted me to represent our side in a shootout."

"That was nice of your foursome to choose you," the wife replied.

"It wasn't our foursome that chose me," the husband said. "It was the other foursome."

And then there was the golfer who liked to plan his second putt before he hit his first drive.

Golf course managers would like only the really good golfers to play. Unfortunately, if only the really good golfers played, the courses would be empty.

"How has your game been today?" one golfer asked another.

"So far, I've hit everything I've aimed for," the other golfer answered.

"I'm impressed," the first golfer said. "How many holes have you played, so far?"

"So far," the second golfer replied, "I've played the driving range."

"What a game. Into the lake, into the rough, into the lake, into the rough . . . . And those were my better drives."

A group of men at a party were bragging about their golf games. A husband joined in. After the party he said to his wife, "Well, I guess now I'm going to have to buy myself some golf clubs and take some lessons."

"How much do you figure your land would be worth if someone wanted to, let's say, buy it and put in a golf course?" a stranger asked a farmer. "At least $50,000 per acre," the farmer replied, sensing an opportunity to make some easy money. "Why? Are you interested in buying?" "No," the stranger replied. "I was just curious. I'm the tax assessor."

"Can I have Friday afternoon off?" an employee asked his boss. "I want to get married."
"Why don't you get married Saturday morning, the way everybody else does?" the boss asked.
"I golf on Saturday mornings," the employee replied.

There are only two kinds of golfers. Those who have fudged on their score card, and those who have not fudged on their score card. Actually, there is probably only one kind of golfer.

A beginner takes some lessons and then heads to the golf course to play his first round. He hits a ball off the tee, sets another ball down and hits it, then sets another ball down and hits it.

He does this about eight times until someone says to him, "You know that ball you just hit, you have to go hit it again."

"Hmmph," the beginner replies. "We didn't have to do that on the practice range."

I know just about everything there is to know about the game of golf. Now if I could only figure out how to play it.

"My husband was quite a legend on this course," one wife said to another. "In fact, that lake over there is named after him."

"Boy, that must have really made him proud."

"Don't know," the wife replied. "They dragged it for three days. Never were able to find him."

I'm a little suspicious of my golf instructor. I went by the course the other day, and *he* was taking lessons.

"I don't seem to be able to get both distance and accuracy with my drives."
"You know what they say, you can have distance, or you can have accuracy, but you can't have both."
"That's not what's bothering me."
"What is bothering you then?"
"I'm not getting either."

"See that man over there," an elderly gentleman said. "He's been golfing for 87 years."
"Can you verify it?" he was asked.
"Sorry, I can't," he replied. "I can only remember golfing with him for 81 years."

A golfer, attempting to reserve a tee time, dialed the wrong number by mistake and got a psychiatrist's office. The receptionist let the doctor know.
"That's strange," she said. "They don't usually telephone until after the game."

"You sliced your ball into that lake over there," one golfer said to another.

"Are you sure I sliced it into the lake?" the other golfer replied. "I've been working on my *draw*."

If you want to discover the difference between good golfers and bad golfers to play with, don't bother adding up their scores, add up their attitudes and their dispositions.

"I was thirty-five years old before I realized I hated golf."

"What happened when you were thirty-five?"

"My first game."

Golfer: "I'm thinking about giving up the game of golf."

Club pro: "I'm feeling safer already."

A golfer was having some difficulty in deciding where to place the responsibility for his poor game, so he blamed his golf equipment half of the time, and the golf course the other half of the time.

"They say that after a while husbands and wives tend to take on similar characteristics," a wife said to her husband as she joined him in the rough to search for a lost golf ball.

We suspected another golfer's drive might have landed in the water when she was asked what kind of lie she had, and she answered, "Murky."

"Strangest thing, Mr. Smith," the tax auditor said. "You claimed that you paid for Bill Jones' round of golf as a business expense on the same day that he claimed your round of golf as a business expense."
Smith thought for a moment. "Maybe we played twice that day."

A golfer returned to his golf instructor. "I don't understand it," he complained. "Bob said you gave him lessons, and now he's shooting par, and I'm still shooting twenty over par. Why is that?"
"You can also shoot par like Bob does," the instructor said, "if you do what he does."
"What's that?"
"Just say you shoot par."

Why does a golfer wear a hat?
So he will have something to talk through after the game.

A husband spent considerable time instructing a wife on how to correct her swing. A minute later, when another wife in their foursome stepped up to the tee to address her ball, he did the same.
"I wish you would tell your husband to keep his nose out of my game," the second wife said to the first after she had completed her drive.
"My husband?" the first wife replied. "I thought he was your husband."

For some reason, golf hasn't been nearly as much fun since I learned the correct way to keep score.

"My wife said that if I really cared about her, I would give up at least one of the activities that I enjoy."
"Oh, oh. Which activity did you decide to give up? Golf?"
"No. Fortunately for me, I don't enjoy golf. However, I do enjoy mowing the lawn and cleaning out the garage. So I gave those up."

A patient said to a psychiatrist, "I think I'm a golfer."

"I know," the psychiatrist replied. "We all do."

A husband talked his wife into going golfing with him. At about the fifth hole he exclaimed, "At least you can quit yawning."

First wife: "My husband just gave me my score, and it's pretty high."
Second wife: "Why don't you tell him to subtract a couple mulligans."
First wife: "Hey, great idea. Honey, on my score, how about subtracting a couple more mulligans."

"There is nothing better than a Saturday and golfing," I once said to another golfer.
He replied, "It sure beats a Tuesday and working."

Women and men talk the same amount on the golf course. Women talk to each other. Men talk to themselves.

It's easy to spot the really slow golfers. They're the ones who are always right in front of you.

Golfers never have difficulty shooting a low score. Shooting a low game, now that could be a problem.

I once shot an ambiguous round of golf. One in the lake, one in the rough, one in the lake, one in the rough, one in the lake, one in . . . .

"My wife says the one positive thing about getting older is that her memory isn't as good as it used to be. She says it allows her to forget the bad golf she played in the past, and instead enjoy the golf she's playing now."
"Really. How far back does her memory loss go?"
"Last hole."

"I have a question," one wife said to another. "When I choose a club, is it still the wrong club, even though my husband isn't here to tell me it's the wrong club?"

A visitor noticed a stranger with a shovel and a rake in the back yard of a friend's house.

"What are you doing?" she asked.

"I'm not quite sure," the stranger replied. "I was playing a round of golf, and I was in a foursome with this lady, and she was having trouble with her swing, and she said that her husband usually helped her but he wasn't there today, so would I mind pretending I was her husband . . . and here I am."

"You have a wonderful swing," an instructor said to a golfer. "You can't hit the ball worth a darn, but you have a wonderful swing."

"I could have told you he'd have trouble golfing," one wife said to another as they watched a husband head into the rough after a ball. "Even in school, he thought the shortest distance between two points was a triangle."

Learning to laugh at our golf games should be a required part of the game, unless of course we happen to be one of those golfers who actually learns the game.

Two non-golfing wives were talking.

"I finally gave in to my husband and watched a golf tournament on T.V.," said one wife, "and I have to tell you, it made me feel better."

"Really?" the other wife answered with considerable surprise.

"Yes," the first wife replied, "but then I always do feel better after taking a nap."

A golf instructor was attempting to help a student with her swing.

"How do you normally hit the ball?" he asked.

"I normally hit it into the rough," the student replied.

"I wish I could afford to play golf," a friend said, admiring a golfer's new set of clubs.

"I wish I could too," the golfer replied with a dejected sigh.

"A dedicated golfer," said a husband, "golfs regardless of the weather."

"So I take it you're still golfing Saturday," his wife responded.

"Of course," he replied, "if it doesn't rain . . . ."

A wife, who had just stepped up to her ball, was talking to herself.

"Line up your feet, bend your knees, keep your head down, mind your back swing, watch your follow through . . . ."

"Do you always talk to yourself like that?" another golfer asked.

"No," she replied. "Usually my husband does it for me, but he's not here today."

One golfer met another who was now a social director on a cruise ship.

"What a surprise seeing you here," the social director said.

"I'm not surprised seeing you," the golfer replied. "Even on the golf course, water seemed to be your calling."

When a golfer hit his ball, it shot across the green and landed on the other side. He hit it back and it did the same thing, landing in the grass on the side he had just left. After doing this several more times without being able to keep his ball on the green, he was asked what he was trying to accomplish. After thinking it over for a moment, he said, "I'm chipping away at my score."

My golf game is like the seasons. It takes me all summer to get it going. Then fall comes and it dies. It rots all winter until spring, then I begin again. Then fall comes . . . .

"I'm always nervous as I stand over my ball for my first shot, but not my second shot."
"It's probably because you relax by the time you get to your ball for your second shot."
"No. It's because I can never find my ball for my second shot."

My husband finally admitted that he's not a great golfer. He now accepts that he's a crappy golfer. Of course, even crappy, he still thinks he's better than anybody else.

"Which sport do you play the most?" a man was asked.
"Golf," he replied.
"Why golf?"
"Same reason I eat spinach."
"And what is that?"
"I hate it, but for some reason I find it's good for me."

I was curious as to why golfers yelled *fore* when they hit a bad shot, so I looked it up. It means *"Toward the front"*. I think we would be better served if they used a version such as *"Toward the side"*, since that's where most shots go. While they're at it, how about other versions such as *"Incoming", "Run for your life", "Cover your head", "Sorry about that"*, and *"If you don't want to get hit by a golf ball, stay out of the parking lot"*.

"You should only golf on those days when you know that you're going to play well."
"But what if I don't know that I'm going to play well?"
"Then don't golf."

No two golfers are alike. If you watch them for a while you'll discover that they're practically all alike.

When you say to a golfer, "How was your game?" and he answers, "Not bad, I got a birdie on one hole," you can pretty well guess what he got on the other seventeen holes that he doesn't want to talk about.

A golfer who regularly shot 110 was asked if he had considered taking lessons.

"What!" he exclaimed. "And screw up my game!"

A clerk in a sporting goods store was preparing equipment to be returned to the manufacturer when he came across a set of golf clubs. On a slip of paper that was attached to the clubs, under reason for returning, someone had written, "Wouldn't hit straight."

"He was just about the slowest person I ever played with," one golfer said about another. "I hit four shots for every one shot he hit, and we still got to the green at the same time."

A golfer hit a hard drive that sliced far off the fairway toward some homes. A second later he heard a crash and the sound of breaking glass.

"What do you think I should do?" he asked another golfer.

"I don't know about you," the other golfer replied, "but I'd be praying I hit something cheap."

"You're the same person who broke a window in my house last year," a homeowner angrily exclaimed as he confronted a golfer in his back yard.

The golfer examined his surroundings, then broke into a wide grin and said, "I knew I had played this course before."

"Play was sure slow today," a golfer muttered as his foursome returned to the club house.

"You're telling me," a golfer who had finished a few foursomes ahead of them agreed. "I've never played such a slow course. It must have taken us six hours to finish."

"Were the foursomes bunched up ahead of you the way they were bunched up ahead of us," the other golfer asked.

"Can't say that they were," the golfer who had finished earlier replied. "No one was ahead of us."

I once asked a bowler if he had ever thought about taking up golf.

He said, "No thank you."

I said, "Why?"

He said, "No air conditioning."

"I was golfing on this course before you were even born," an old timer said to a duffer.

"I thought you were a little slow," the duffer answered.

A golfer telephoned to get a tee time.

"I'm sorry sir," the clerk informed him, "but it's been raining for three days solid, and the course is flooded under three feet of water."

"Yeah, yeah," the golfer replied. "But is it playable?"

Two men were discussing their golf game from the previous Saturday, in which they had played thirty-six holes and then enjoyed a considerable amount of good conversation with other golfers in the club house.

"How did you enjoy yourself?" one of them asked.

"I had a really great time," the other replied, "except for all the cussing and fuming and complaining."

"I don't recall hearing any cussing and fuming and complaining," the first golfer said.

The second golfer grimaced. "That's because you didn't come home with me."

It had been raining steady for the entire day. Rivers were overflowing their banks, roads were washed out, and citizens were being warned not to venture out unless absolutely necessary. As the four golfers stared at a large tree that had blown down and was lying across the only entrance to the golf course, one of them said, "I think they could be right about us not trying to go anywhere. We might as well just stay here and play another eighteen."

Golf is a funny game. When we first begin playing we try to picture ourselves getting a hole in one. After a few games we try to picture ourselves hitting the golf course.

"Just think, a hundred years ago our ancestors used to plow these fields," a golfer said as he flailed away on a fairway that was in less than ideal condition.

"I'll bet they never guessed that a hundred years later someone would turn it into a golf course," another golfer offered.

"Oh?" the first golfer responded as he took another swipe at his ball. "Did they turn it into a golf course????"

"What's the name of your book?" a golfer asked an author.

"How To Learn Golf In Five Easy Lessons," the author answered.

"I'll give you this much," the golfer replied, "you certainly have a good imagination."

A visitor was watching a grounds keeper hitting golf balls on a small town course. He couldn't help but notice the man's remarkable accuracy. In a manner reminiscent of a rifle marksman preparing for target practice, the grounds keeper would wet a finger, run it along the blade of the club, take aim, and then with a swish and a whack, barely miss a pesky rodent that was digging a hole in the fairway two hundred yards away. After witnessing the accuracy several more times, the visitor approached

"With the golfing skills you possess," he said, "you should be playing professionally."

"Already tried it," the grounds keeper replied, "but I had to give it up."

"Why?" the visitor asked. "Weren't you good enough?"

"Wasn't that," the grounds keeper said. "I did O.K. golfing, but they don't allow hunting on those big city courses."

The main difference between my golf game and my wife's golf game: I have trouble deciding which clubs to take. She has trouble deciding which clothes to wear.

"When I golf, I like to compete against myself. For instance, if I golfed 90 last week, I try to golf 89 this week."
"So, what's the problem?"
"Lately, I keep losing."

"How come your teenage son has suddenly developed such an interest in golf? He never wanted to play before."
"It's because his father promised to teach him a part of the game today that he has never let him do up until now."
"What's that?"
"Drive the golf cart."

We decided a golfer, who had just finished his round, had perhaps spent a little too much time in the rough when we asked, "How are the fairways on this course?"
And he replied, "What fairways?"

Two golfers met on the first tee.
"How come you're golfing on a Wednesday?" asked one.
"My company went on strike," said the other.
"Oh, I'm sorry to hear that," said the first. "Do you think it will last long?"
"I sure hope so," answered the striker.

When asked how long their golf course was, a club pro replied, "Oh, about 7000 yards as the crow flies. A little longer as the ball flies."

You can tell when a professional has hit a good drive off the tee, because he starts walking.
You can tell when an amateur has hit a good drive off the tee, because he remains there and admires it.

"I'm just as good at golf today as I was thirty years ago," an elderly golfer informed his fellow golfers.
"Amazing," one of the other golfers responded.
"Not as amazing as you think," the elderly golfer's wife replied. "He wasn't any good thirty years ago either."

"I was in the rough when I saw a flying saucer tangled in the underbrush and two little green men trying to get out," a golfer exclaimed.

"What did you do?" he was asked.

"I left them there," he answered. "I was having enough trouble getting myself out."

Two professional golfers were driving through a small town and decided to play a round at the local golf course. They were paired with two duffers who didn't recognize them.

"How are you doing?" one of the duffers asked after nine holes.

"Two under so far," one of the professionals said without bothering to look at his score card.

"Me too," the other professional added.

The duffer who had asked the question leaned toward his partner and said, "Keep an eye on these two. I think they could be cheating."

A disgruntled golfer was overheard saying, "The thing I hate most about golf is having to hit that little ball. The thing I have the most difficulty with is hitting it straight. The most frustrating thing is getting it into the hole. I think I'll take up soccer."

"How come your ball always ends up in this rough?" a golfer was asked.

"Easy," he replied. "Do you see that fairway over there?"

"Yes."

"And do you see that other fairway over there?"

"Yes."

"Well, I just aim for one of those fairways, and here I am."

A beginner was on the driving range. Her golf balls were flying in every direction.

"How long do you think it will take me to become a golfer?" she asked in frustration.

"It takes a while to get there," the pro replied.

After many more shots that were also scattered across the driving range, she exclaimed again, "Just how long is it going to take me to become a golfer anyway?"

"Don't worry, you'll get there," said the pro.

A bucket of golf balls later, and many more shots that were scattered all over the driving range, she couldn't take it any more, and let forth with some choice words unbecoming a lady.

The pro nodded his head in approval, and with a broad smile replied, "I think you might have just become a golfer."

"Golfing lets me feel that I'm getting back to nature."
"Because you're outdoors?"
"Because I'm usually up to my behind in tall grass and water."

"My plans for Saturday are to mow the lawn and then go golfing."
"Does your wife know about your plans?"
"She knows about the mowing the lawn part."

A father took his young son golfing with him. As they waited their turn on the first tee, the boy asked, "What is the most difficult thing to do in golf?"
"The most difficult thing to do in golf is to hit what you're aiming for," his father answered. Then he stepped up to the tee and drove his ball into the side of a house beside the fairway.
"Wow!" the boy exclaimed. "Let's see if you can hit another one."

You might suspect you're a slow golfer when you look ahead and wonder where everybody went. Then you look behind, and you find out.

It's amazing, how four different golfers, with four different clubs and four different swings, can hit four different golf balls into the same lake.

"A lousy three feet," a golfer muttered. "That's all that was between my golf ball and a decent lie for my second shot to the green."

"Oh," another golfer sympathized. "Is that how far your ball was from the fairway?"

"No," the first golfer replied. "That's how far my ball was from the shore."

"I used to practice a lot," one golfer said to another, "then I decided just to get golf clubs with a bigger sweet spot."

"I'm not talking to my husband."

"Why not?"

"Because he refuses to yell *fore* when I hit a bad shot."

"Why don't you just yell *fore* yourself?"

"I do."

"Then what does he yell?"

"Run for your lives."

I finally improved my aim. The roughs and the lakes are much easier to hit now.

First duffer: "I shot a hundred and twenty-five today, but it didn't look so good, so I rounded my score down a little."
Second duffer: "What number did you round it down to? A hundred and twenty?"
First duffer: "Ninety."

Why is it: When I use a new golf ball, I hit the lake. When I use a water ball, I hit the fairway.

A golfer was asked why he took up the game. He replied, "It sure wasn't for the conversation."

"How is your husband's golf game coming?" "Much better. Sometimes he doesn't even start cussing until his second or third shot."

Why is it, the more we think about keeping our golf ball out of a lake, the more certain we can be that it will land there.

I like the off season. I telephoned the golf course and asked what time I could tee off, and they said, what time can you be here?

"What do you plan to do when you retire?"
"Go golfing."
"And then what?"
"Go golfing."

"My wife never has to worry about hitting anybody with a golf ball," a husband said as his wife prepared to tee off.
"Is she that good?" another golfer asked.
"No," he replied, "it's not that. When they see her on the tee box, they run for cover."

"Well, what quality of golfer do you think I'll make?" a young man asked after finishing his lesson.
"I was just asking myself the same question," his golf instructor answered.

You can always tell a golfer who embellishes his score. The score keeps changing.

"To me," a wife said, "a golf shop is a place to get a tee time. To my husband, it's a toy store."

Spring is that time of year when everything on the golf course blossoms . . . except my game.

A wife was watching her father-in-law and her husband practice on the driving range.

"My father-in-law is handing his golfing skills down to his son," she said to another golfer beside her.

After watching them for a few minutes, the golfer remarked, "I think your father-in-law must have another son he hasn't been telling you about."

"How do you know when you're playing too slow?"

"When the golf balls from the group behind reach the green before yours does."

You might begin to suspect you'll never be a professional golfer when someone says, "You need more practice," and you've already been practicing for twenty years.

The crazy thing about golf is, you can miss six months of playing and it won't affect your game. You can miss two weeks and it will.

"A picture is worth a thousand words," one golfer said to another as a ball sailed into a lake. "Personally," the golfer who had hit the ball replied, "I prefer the thousand words."

"I shot par going out, and seven over coming back," one golfer said to another.
"Kind of makes you wonder why you bothered coming back," the other golfer replied.

A golfer, describing his shot, exclaimed, "Did you see that? My ball landed right on the green, and you missed it."
"Don't worry," another golfer replied. "I'm sure that someday you'll hit another green."

A wife was asked if she ever gave herself less strokes on her score card than she really had.
"No," she answered. "My husband does that for me."

"In golf," a golf pro said, "the most important skill to maintain is a good consistent swing."
"And just how do I go about maintaining a good consistent swing?" a student asked.
"Search me," the pro replied. "I've never seen anyone maintain one."

Who said, "There is no such thing as a bad golfer?"
"The owners of the golf course."

"Keep an eye on that fellow over there," one golfer said to another. "I know for a fact that he doesn't count all his strokes."
"How do you know?" the other golfer asked.
"Because I taught him how to play," the first golfer replied.

"Give me one good reason why I can't shoot golf in the seventies," one golfer said to another.
"I can give you more than one good reason," the other golfer replied, "I can give you thirteen good reasons."
"Where do you get thirteen reasons?"
"I wasn't including your putter."

After spending millions of dollars on research to determine whether the golf ball or the golf club was more instrumental in lowering golf scores, a manufacturer reached the following conclusion. It was the golfer.

You say you've never heard a golfer swear? Try watching one very carefully as he goes into the rough after a ball. Those lip movements you see aren't him complimenting himself on making a good shot.

"Wow, what a challenging golf course," a golfer exclaimed. "I was able to use almost every club in my bag."
"That's great," the other golfer replied, "really great. Now let's see how we do on to the second hole."

"Why is that golfer continuing to choke down on his seven iron like that?"
"If you take a look at where his last shot landed, and then look more carefully at him, you'll notice he's not continuing to choke down on his seven iron, he's just choking it."

"A birdie in the round is worth five in the lake," a golfer sighed philosophically.

"Don't you mean a bird in the hand is worth two in the bush?" another golfer said.

"Don't play much, do you," the first golfer responded.

Wife: "Does it count as a stroke if I miss the ball?"

Husband: "That's three."

Most of the best golfers in the world are respected, not just because they are good, but because they are good for the game.

I began to suspect my new oversized club might be too big when I fell over during my back swing.

If we didn't know what golf is, and someone said to us, I want you to take this stick here, and this little ball, and using the stick, hit the ball into a hole five hundred yards away, that you can't even see, except for another stick that is sticking out of the hole, we would think they were crazy.

I think my aim must be getting better. During my golf game last Saturday morning, I hit my ball into a neighboring yard beside the seventh fairway, and the owner said to me, "I haven't seen you for a while."

A golfer hit yet another ball into a lake.
"You're not a very good golfer," another golfer scoffed.
"Thank goodness for that," the golfer who had hit his shot into the lake replied. "I'd hate to be playing like this if I were a good golfer."

A golfer was having difficulty getting a tee time at the local course.
"Just leave it to me," another golfer said. "I know the pro there. I'll get you one. All you have to do is call to confirm."
The golfer did as he was instructed and called, only to be told that his tee time was a half hour before the sun came up.
A week later, when he ran into the other golfer again, he said, "I thought you said you know the pro there."
"I do," the other golfer replied. "Didn't you notice the early tee time I got you?"

"I think my wife's golf game is getting better. It only took her one shot with her five iron to get out of that rough."

"How does that make her better?"

"She went in there with three other clubs."

"How has everything been going this morning?" a golfer was asked.

"For the most part," she replied, "everything has been going into that lake over there."

A golfer who had not played well was muttering and cursing to himself as he walked off the golf course.

Seeing how upset he was, one of his companions said, "You know, if you have that much trouble with the game, perhaps you should consider giving it up."

"What!" he screamed. "And miss all the fun!"

"Gosh, darn . . . ."

"That's awfully nice of you not to swear, just because your ball rolled into the lake."

"If my ball wants to get sweared at, it's going to have to go a lot farther into the lake than that."

"Are you absolutely sure this is the golfer that broke the window in your house?" the judge asked the home owner.

"Yes I am your honor," the home owner answered.

"How can you be so sure?"

"Well, first of all, I saw his ball come through my window."

"It could have been another golfer's ball."

"Then I saw him climb over my fence and begin searching for it."

"It does look suspicious," the judge sympathized, "but he could have been helping another golfer look for his ball."

"Then I saw him examine the hole in my window and stare through it looking for his ball."

"But he still might have been helping another golfer look for his ball."

"Then he broke into my house to get the ball."

"I'm sorry," the judge said. "We might be able to get him for breaking and entering, but we still don't know that it was his ball."

"Then he took his next shot from the middle of my kitchen floor," the home owner revealed.

"I think we might have him," the judge declared.

Duffer: Any golfer other than ourselves.

One after another, four golfers in a foursome drove their golf balls into the rough.

"What you guys need," a member of another foursome suggested, "is a good golf instructor."

To which one of them sheepishly answered. "I am their golf instructor."

A speech and a golf game have something in common. The best ones finish early.

A professional golfer, when he wasn't competing on the golf course, practiced eight hours a day, seven days a week.

When asked why he became a golfer, he said, "It beats working."

A first time golfer made a hole in one with his very first shot on the first hole. After waiting for everyone else to finish on the green, he made another hole in one with his first shot on the second hole. After waiting again for everyone to finish on the green, be picked up his ball and began to walk off the course.

"Where are you going?" another golfer asked.

"This game is no fun," he replied.

After being beaten quite badly by an elderly golfer in their foursome, one of the younger players offered up an excuse to save face.

"I would have played a lot better," he said, "but I'm playing with hand-me-down clubs from my father."

"What a coincidence," the elderly gentleman replied. "So am I."

Two men of the cloth were playing golf. One couldn't help but notice that the other, after hitting an exceptionally good shot, would say a quick prayer over his club before returning it to his bag.

This went on for several holes until the reverend hit a drive into a lake. He looked at his ball in the water, said a few words over his club, and then jammed it back into his bag.

"Why did you pray over that club when it hit such a bad shot?" the other reverend asked.

"I wasn't praying over it," the first reverend answered. "I was giving it the last rites."

A wife, watching her husband on the practice range, commented, "He has more swings than a city park."

I have found the most difficult chore in golf is getting a tee time.
The second most difficult chore is getting out of bed at five o'clock in the morning to make it to the tee time.

Why did the golfer cross the road?
To get to his second drive.

Sometimes in golf we can play a really good round and still have a poor score. Sometimes we can play a really poor round and still have a good score. It just depends on which way the ball bounces. The main reason some golfers enjoy golf so much in spite of the bounces, while others don't, is their attitude and their love of the game. Golf is a lot like life.

One way to tell where other golfers have golfed is to examine the names on towels that hang from their golf bags. Just last Saturday I saw golfers who had played at Saint Andrews, Pebble Beach, Augusta, East Cove Health Club, Harry's Gym, Holiday Inn, Honey Cove Motel, and Mom's Bless Everyone In This House Kitchen.

A wife, not being familiar with the game of golf, was happy when her husband said he would be home right after the nineteenth hole.

"Watch this," a golfer said. "I've trained my dog to fetch my golf clubs. Fetch me a wedge," he commanded the dog.
"That's nothing," scoffed a listener. "Any fool can teach his dog to bring a golf club."
"Do you want your sand wedge or your pitching wedge?" asked the dog.

A golfer went to a golf pro for lessons. After watching him take a few swings, the pro commented, "Your game is really bad."
Disgusted, the golfer went to another golf pro. After watching him take a few swings, this pro said, "Your game is really terrible."
The golfer said, "I'm going back to the first golf pro."
The second pro asked, "Why?"
The golfer responded, "He has a higher opinion of my game."

Golf buffet: You only play the holes you like.

The swing is probably the most honest part of our entire game. We would like to lie about it, but we can't.

A really good golfer is a really bad golfer who can still have a really good time even when he's playing really bad.

Golfers can be divided into three categories, good golfers, bad golfers, and bad golfers who believe they are good golfers.

I find one of the biggest problems with an early fall blizzard is finding my golf ball.

"Part of my game was good and part of my game was bad," a husband said to his wife. "First of all, I shot 112 and spent most of the day in the rough . . . except for the hole where I fell into the lake retrieving a ball. Then I left my new putter on a green, and when I went back to get it, it was gone. And if that wasn't enough, I lost a dollar bet on every hole."

"And," his wife said, "what was the bad part?"

A golfer was asked if she could fade the ball.
She answered, "No."
Then she was asked if she could draw the ball.
Again she answered, "No."
Finally she was asked if there was any shot she could make.
She smiled. "I have a pretty good mulligan."

"I got a new set of golf clubs for my husband," one wife said to another.
"I don't think I could get that much for mine," the other wife answered.

A husband could be heard muttering to himself in the garage.
A visitor, after listening to the tantrum, said, "If he gets upset that easy, he'd better never take up golf."
"Where do you think he just came from?" the wife replied.

"When my wife began playing golf, I did a lot to help her with her nervousness."
"Really. What did you do?"
"I stayed home."

"Does your husband play golf?"
"Not the way he does it."

I bought a set of those new golf clubs with the flexible shafts. And just in time. My body has stopped bending.

"How much is a game of golf worth today?" a golfer was asked.
"About ten dollars."
"But your clubs alone cost you two thousand."
"That's true."
"And your golf balls cost forty dollars a pack."
"True."
"And your golfing attire must have set you back several hundred dollars."
"True again."
"Then how can you say a game of golf is worth only ten dollars?"
"Because when I asked the club pro what he thought my game was worth, that's what he said, about ten dollars."

And then there was the man who was saving his money for a rainy day. He was going golfing.

"What are you doing?" one wife asked another who was throwing golf clubs into a lake.

"My wifely duties," the second wife answered. "I was doing the laundry, and my husband said that as long as I had the water going anyway, I could clean his golf clubs for him. This is the rinse cycle."

A golfer accidentally subtracted three strokes for a hole on her score card. "It's all right," she said. "I accidentally added a stroke on another hole. It evens out."

"Where did you get the black eye?"

"From my ball getting a lucky bounce onto the green."

"What does your ball getting a lucky bounce onto the green have to do with your black eye?"

"I was given the black eye by the golfer I got the lucky bounce off."

A psychiatrist had a patient who thought he was a golfer. It took a lot of work but he finally convinced him he was a bowler. He's much happier now.

"Wouldn't it be nice if we could get corporate sponsors like the professionals do," one duffer said to another as they prepared to hit their first drives of the afternoon.

"I already have a corporate sponsor," the other duffer replied.

"Who?"

"My company. They think I'm working."

"The manager of this golf course used to work for a grocery store, and he's utilized his retail experience to make some changes."

"I'd like to meet him."

"I'm sorry, he's out on the course."

"Where on the course?"

"The fourteenth aisle."

"How come all your shots are going into that lake over there?" a golfer asked sarcastically.

"I don't know," the other golfer replied just as sarcastically. "After all, I was aiming for that rough over there."

One library put their golf instruction books in the entertainment section.

"Did you just hit your ball into the lake?" one golfer asked another.

"No," the first golfer answered. "I hit it into the rough. It had to roll into the lake."

"Do you really think all that cussing and swearing is going to bring your golf ball out of the lake?" an indignant bystander asked.

"No," the golfer replied, "but it sure makes it being in there a lot easier to accept."

"Thank you," a golfer said to a bystander. "I appreciate your honesty."

"Appreciate her honesty about what?" another golfer asked when the bystander had moved along.

"Oh nothing," the first golfer answered. "She was just saying what a terrific golfer I am."

"Every time I arrive home from golf I find my wife in the arms of another man," a golfer confided to a fellow golfer. "What do you think I should do?"

"I really don't know," the other golfer replied, "unless . . . perhaps get a later tee time . . . ?"

A husband and wife were standing beside the first tee discussing the type of day they could expect on the course. The husband was not being very optimistic about his game.

"Remember that a journey of a thousand miles begins with the first step," another golfer who overheard their conversation offered.

"You've watched my husband golf before, haven't you," the wife replied.

A couple was held up leaving the golf course.

"Stick 'em up and hand me your golf clubs," the robber demanded.

"Don't you mean, hand me your money?" the wife said.

"Look lady," the bandit growled, "you do what you want and I'll do what I want."

An old timer was asked if there was any part of his golf game that had deteriorated as he grew older.

"Yes," he replied. "I can't hit the ball as far as I used to."

Then he was asked if there was any part of his game that had improved.

"Yes," he replied. "Now I can find my ball."

"I hate this game," a golfer complained. "I never have any fun, and it costs me a fortune."

"Just think how much it could cost you if you *were* having fun," his wife answered.

Professional golfers never lose their golf balls. But then, if I had a hundred thousand people watching my drives, I wouldn't lose them either.

"You're going to see a 360 degree change in my game this year," a golfer promised.

Two other golfers were listening. "Do you really believe what he says?" asked one.

"First you have to consider where 360 degrees will take him," the other replied.

"Could you maybe move off the green," a ranger said to some poky golfers who were discussing their games and filling in their score cards rather than leaving the green after sinking their putts.

"Why?" one of the golfers asked.

"Because all those people behind you can't golf," the ranger answered.

"If they can't golf, then why did they take up the game?" the poky golfer responded.

You know you're getting a putter for Christmas when your children ask if they can measure the distance from your hands to the floor.

Why is it, every time I hit a golf ball into the rough, I find a golf ball, but it's never mine.

"Looks like a difficult lie you have there."
"Oh, it's not too difficult."
"Do you think you should maybe take a penalty stroke and a drop?"
"No, I don't think so."
"Don't you think you might be just a little out of bounds?"
"I don't think so."
"I really think you should reconsider trying to take your shot from that lie?"
"Look, I can make this shot, and why do you keep asking me all these questions anyway?"
"Because you're in my flower bed."

"I love this game," a golfer said. "In fact, I could play forever."
A golfer from the following foursome, who was listening, replied, "So I've noticed."

"I once read that it took a professional golfer two years to perfect a new swing," one golfer said to another.

"Heck, I perfect a new swing every time I play," the other golfer responded, "sometimes two or three of them."

Golfers were comparing their swings. One of them described his swing as being very loyal.

"No matter how many times I hook and slice my drives," he said, "it never leaves me."

One golf manufacturer brags that it's excellent line of golf clubs will give the straightest drives you have ever seen. They also sell a pretty good line of ball retrievers.

"It's important to know what each club is for," a husband said to his wife. "For instance, for this shot, the proper club to use is a five iron."

After watching her ball sail into a lake, his wife replied, "O.K., we know what that club is for. Now, which club should I use if I want to hit that little round piece of grass down there with the hole in it."

I would never cheat in golf. I might take a mulligan or two, but I would never cheat.

"Tell me about your golf game this morning," a husband was asked at a Saturday night party.

"I'd like to," he said, "but I can't."

"Why not?"

"Sore ankle."

"You couldn't play golf because of a sore ankle?"

"I played O.K., but talking about it gives me a sore ankle."

"How can talking about your golf game at a party give you a sore ankle?"

"That's where my wife kicks me."

A beginner asked a golfer if he could tell the type of shot he made by the sound he heard.

"Possibly," the golfer answered. "If you hear a splash, your ball could be in the water. If you hear a whack, it could be in the trees. If you hear a crash you can be pretty sure you hit a house, if you hear a nice clear smooth swish . . . ."

"It means I hit a good shot . . . ?" the beginner said optimistically.

"It could," the golfer replied. "It could also mean you missed your ball."

Wife to husband on fourteenth fairway: "Don't yell at me. I didn't hit your ball into the lake."

Golfers are funny. If they're doing really well, they're noisy. If they're doing really poorly, they're noisy. If they're doing just O.K., they don't make a sound.

The bad part about my golf game is, I always seem to choose the wrong club. The good part is, it doesn't seem to make much difference.

There are two groups on Sunday morning who believe in miracles. One group is in Church. The other group is about to hit their golf balls off the first tee.

A bogey and a birdie are sometimes about as different as a golf game and a score card.

I became so tired of losing golf balls that I gave up the game and became a bowler. It's very difficult to lose a bowling ball.

A student showed up at a golf clinic in time to hear the instructor say, "There's nothing to golf. All you have to do is get your mind and your body working as one, like you do in college."
The student sighed, "Oh, oh . . . ."

"I think you might have finally found your game," an instructor said to a golfer.
"Nuts," the golfer exclaimed. "I was hoping I might find someone else's game."

"What does your husband's golf bag look like?" one wife asked another.
"Think of your purse," the other wife answered. "You don't really know what's in there, but you don't throw any of it away either because you're afraid you might need it someday . . . ?"
"Yes . . . ?"
"Well, that's what his golf bag looks like."

"What is your husband writing?" a wife was asked.
"An ad to get rid of his stress," she answered.
"How can an ad possibly get rid of stress?"
"He's selling his golf clubs."

"I watched a trick shot golfer the other day," a wife said. "He could hit a ball 50 yards over the rough, and then draw it back and land it in the fairway."

"I can do that," her husband responded, "except for the landing in the fairway part."

"How are you doing?" one golfer asked another.

"Not bad," the second golfer replied. "So far I've had eleven pars and a birdie."

"Wow!" the first golfer exclaimed. "I'm impressed. I don't meet too many golfers who have a game that good."

"Oh, I didn't know you meant my game," the second golfer said. "I thought you meant since I began golfing."

A woman took up golfing in the spring. Her new set of clubs had yellow grips. She wanted to know what colors were available for the other three seasons.

A new golfer, after shooting 148, said, "You know, I'm better at this than I thought I was going to be."

"My wife doesn't like to see me enjoy myself golfing."

"Does she insist that you stay home?"

"No. She insists on coming with me."

"My wife and I do everything together."

"Even golf?"

"Even golf."

"When did you start golfing together?"

"When she said, I don't care what we do, but we're doing it together. We can either golf together, or we can clean up the house together, or we can go shopping together, but we're doing it together."

"How many strokes did you have on that hole?" one golfer asked another.

The other golfer began counting the strokes on her fingers. When she was finished with one hand, she switched to the other.

"My gosh," the golfer who had asked the question exclaimed. "Are you saying you need the fingers on both hands to count your strokes?"

The other golfer didn't say anything. She just scowled and moved back to the fingers on her first hand to continue the count.

"I don't understand why I keep missing the fairway," a new golfer said. "I didn't have any difficulty hitting the driving range."

Husband: "On the first hole I shot a par."
Wife: "Yawn . . . ."
Husband: "On the second hole I shot a birdie."
Wife: "Yawn . . . ."
Husband: "On the third hole I got another par."
Wife: "Yawn . . . ."
Husband: "On the fourth hole I hit a ball into a lake and fell in trying to get it.
Wife: "That hole I'd like to hear about."

"I just want to make a tee time, not buy the golf course," a golfer exclaimed when he saw the price he had to pay for a round.
"Don't be ridiculous," the clerk replied. "You wouldn't have to pay this much for the golf course."

It is not difficult to offer advice to another golfer on how to play the game, choose the right club, or putt on the right line. Now, if we could just do it for ourselves.

"My golf instructor has not been able to find one fault in my game," a golfer bragged.
"Really?" another golfer asked. "Which one?"

"My husband has to decide whether to give up bowling or golfing," a wife said, "because he doesn't have time for both."
"Which game does he play the best?" the other wife asked.
"That's his problem. He's equally good at both sports."
"Really? What is his score in each?"
"117."

"The main difference between you and me," a golf course owner said to a golfer, "is you count your score, while I count your money."

"What do you think of my golf game?" a proud golfer asked.
"I've seen worse," another golfer informed him.
"What do you mean, you've seen worse?" the golfer replied indignantly.
"O.K., so I haven't seen worse," the other golfer replied.

"My husband has played golf in twenty-seven different countries."

"Did it help his game?"

"No, but he did learn twenty-seven new ways to describe it."

"I don't care how cute it sounds," a husband said to his wife. "When you call for our tee time, stop telling them you want tees for two."

"I shot seven over," a wife informed her husband.

Her husband raised an eyebrow and asked, "Seven over what?"

A golfer with a split personality thought he was a foursome. The golf course was really good about it. They only charged him for three.

"I heard that golfing is a good place to meet men," one young woman golfer said to another.

"I'm not so sure," the other replied as they watched the men scatter in search of their errant shots.

Wife: "I'm looking for a new set of golf clubs for my husband."

Golf Pro: "We have several new lines that we can customize to fit just about any type of game. For instance, this set is called the straight arrows, this set is called the long rifles, this set is called the sure shots, this set is called the . . . ."

Wife: "Do you have anything in a twelve-gauge shotgun?"

Student: "What do you think my chances are of getting a hole in one after finishing my lessons?"

Golf pro: "About one in seven million."

Student: "How come you tell me one in seven million, and my last golf instructor told me one in eight million?"

Golf pro: "I'm a better instructor."

A golfer spent many thousands of dollars for lessons that barely improved his game.

"Why, why, why?" he complained to the pro who had given the lessons. "Why did my game change such a small amount after spending so much money?"

The pro thought about it for a moment before he replied. "Inflation . . . ???"

"Ah, Saturday, golf with my husband, ballet with my daughter, soccer practice with my son, and then finally, reading a good book . . . ."

"How do you find the time?"

"Easy. I drop my husband off at golf, I drop my daughter off at ballet, I drop my son off at soccer, and then I read a good book."

"My husband and I had played almost halfway through the seventeenth hole in our golf game last Saturday before he even bothered talking to me."

"That's terrible of him. What did he say?"

"Don't get excited. The water's only up to your waist."

A salesman was asked to explain the secret of his success.

"Well," he said, "I probably owe much of my success to hitting all those poor golf shots and missing all those easy putts when I'm out with a client."

"Are you saying you throw the game to get a sale?" his listener exclaimed.

"Not at all," the golfer replied. "Fortunately, I'm just not a very good golfer."

By using a new advanced computer technology program, my golf instructor was able to show me the score I could expect after I perfected my swing. I liked it. According to the computer, I would be 37 under par.

"I don't understand it," a husband said. "I taught my wife everything I know about golf, and she still can't hit a ball straight."

"Where'd you get the bump on your head?"
"Golfing."
"Hit by a ball?"
"Hit by the wife. I was giving her lessons and stood a little too close to her back swing. It was an accident . . . I think."

Husband to wife: "If you knew the first time you laid eyes on that golf pro that he was the worst instructor in the world, why on earth did you take lessons from him for six months?"

Every time we see one golfer, he tells us about a different once in a lifetime shot he made.

After slicing and hooking for many years, I've reached the point in my golf game where I don't get upset as long as my ball goes straight. I don't even care how far or in which direction, as long as it goes straight.

A husband who had been an air force pilot was teaching his wife to golf.

"Just imagine every fairway to be a clock," he said. "The tee is at six, the green is at twelve, the edges of the fairway are at eleven and one, and the roughs are at ten and two."

"Well," he asked after she hit her shot, "is your ball at twelve?"

"No," she answered.

"Is it at eleven or one?" he asked.

"No," she answered again.

"Then is it at ten or two?" he asked.

"No," she answered once more.

"Then where is it?" he demanded.

After some hesitation, she slowly replied, "I think it might be on another clock."

If you think that human beings are the only animals that can laugh, visit a golf course, and listen very carefully.

Two golfers are talking.
One golfer says, "I only have one shot."
The other golfer asks, "Don't you ever slice your ball into the rough?"
The first golfer replies, "Yes. That's my one shot."

One golfer can always find something to blame when she hits a poor drive. Last weekend she was heard blaming her tees.

A professional golfer decided to give up the game and become a minister.
"Has the ministry affected your language on the golf course?" he was asked.
"Not too much," the pastor answered. "I just have to choose my words a little more carefully."

"I have pain every time I do this," a patient said as he twisted his body, threw his arms back and over his head, contorted his knees, and jerked his body forward.
"Then just stop doing it," the doctor advised.
"I would," the patient answered, "but how else am I going to hit my golf ball."

"I think your golf game just might be improving," a husband said to his wife. "Even your slices are looking better today."

"My husband made two hundred feet with his five iron this morning."
"That doesn't seem like much."
"He would have made more, but his club hit a tree."

"I think I need new golf clubs," a golfer said.
"It's not the clubs," another golfer reminded him. "It's the idiot that's holding the clubs."
"Don't you call my golf bag an idiot," the golfer replied.

"My husband says we're playing today with the worst, bad tempered, obnoxious golfer in the whole world," one wife said to another.
"My husband told me the same thing," the other wife replied.
"Here comes my husband now," the first wife said.
"My husband is with him," the second wife answered.

"How many strokes does it take to complete this course?" one golfer asked another.
"It depends," answered the other golfer.
"On who's playing?"
"On who's keeping score."

"My five iron's bent," a husband complained.
"That's funny," his wife replied. "It was O.K. yesterday when I was working in the garden."

My golf game was so bad I decided to learn some new techniques. I learned a new golf swing, a new putting stroke, a new chipping style . . . . Now I have two bad golf swings, two bad putting strokes, two bad chipping styles . . . .

"I seem to be having trouble with my game," a golfer said. "Do you think you can help me?" The instructor, after watching him hit some balls, said, "Let me put it this way. Do you remember the nursery rhyme about Humpty Dumpty?"
"Yes," the golfer answered. "Some egg fell off a wall, and all the king's horses, and all the king's men, couldn't put it back together again. So?"
"So," the instructor replied, "that's your game."

"Why is your wife so excited?"

"She just hit a ball into that rough over there."

"Why would that make her excited?"

"She cleared the lake to get it there."

"How many perfectionists does it take to fill out a golf score card?"

"Only one, but he does it over, and over, and over, and over . . . ."

"Let's say you took four shots to get to the green and four more putts to sink your ball," a young golfer said. "What would your score be?"

"Par," an old time golfer replied.

"It's obvious that you don't know a lot about arithmetic," the young golfer scoffed.

"And it's obvious that you don't know a lot about golfers," the old timer scoffed back.

"You haven't been able to do with your swing what I've been trying to teach you," a golf instructor informed his student.

"If I could do with my swing what you've been trying to teach me," the student replied, "I wouldn't need you, would I?"

"Just think," one golfer said to another. "In some countries they don't even have golf."
"Lucky people," the other golfer answered.

One married man asked another married man if he would like to go golfing.
"I'm the boss in my house," the other man blustered. "I can golf anytime I want to."
"Well?" the first married man said, "Do you want to?"
"Just hold on one minute," the second married man answered, glancing toward his wife, "while I go see."

There always seems to be a tree between my ball and the green. I can't remember the last time I saw a tree between my ball and a lake.

A group of golfers were doing a little bragging in the clubhouse.
"Some of my shots go 300 yards and some go 350 yards," one of them said.
"And how's your short game?" another golfer asked.
"That is my short game," the braggart replied.

"I finally discovered why I haven't been able to hit a green," a husband said to his wife.

"Oh?" she answered.

"Yes," he continued. "The optometrist said that as I'm getting older, my eyesight is getting poorer."

"But you couldn't hit a green even when you did have good eyesight," his wife informed him.

"I know," he said, "but I didn't have a reason then. Now I do."

"My girlfriend told me that if I didn't give her an engagement ring, she wouldn't be seeing me any more."

"What did you do?"

"I bought a new set of golf clubs and a membership at a golf resort."

"Why would you do that?"

"I figured I'd be needing something to do, since I wouldn't be dating."

"I don't think you mean you have golfer's elbow," a doctor said to a tennis player. "I think you mean you have tennis elbow."

"No," the tennis player replied. "I'm sure I have golfer's elbow. All my serves have been slicing."

"My shoulder hurts and I'm shooting a hundred and twelve," a golfer complained to a doctor.
"I'm afraid I'm going to have to recommend something really drastic for it," the doctor said.
"Is my shoulder that bad?" the worried golfer asked.
"Your shoulder's going to be O.K.," the doctor replied. "I'm talking about your golf game."

Have you noticed, no matter how poor a golfer's game has been, it always seems to improve when he's sitting in the clubhouse afterwards.

"I don't know what to say about my golf game."
"Probably the less, the better."

First golfer: "What did you get on that last hole?"
Second golfer: "I don't like to tell other people my score, because they never believe me."
First golfer: "I'll believe you."
Second golfer: "O.K., I got a birdie."
First golfer: "But you must have taken at least eight shots."
Second golfer: "What did I tell you . . . ."

The golf course was really busy today. On some tees the golfers were lined up three, sometimes four deep.

I gave up golf because my game wasn't compatible with the fairways. The fairways were 75 yards wide and my game was 250 yards wide.

Golf is a lot like marriage. When it's good, it's really good, but when it's bad .... Come to think of it, it's not like marriage at all.

Why is it, when other golfers drive their golf balls into the rough or a lake, it's just a game. When we drive our own golf ball into the rough or a lake, it's a dirty, rotten, stupid, crappy, lowdown, miserable, waste of time, no good game.

"There is absolutely nothing I can think of to improve your golf swing," a golf instructor said to a golfer.
"You mean my golf swing is perfect?"
"I didn't say that. I said there was nothing I could think of that would improve it."

A slice is just a perfect drive
That moves a little right,
Unless it turns into a hook
And takes a leftward flight.

"My wife asked me to give up golf for marriage, so I did."
"But you're golfing now, and you just got married this morning."
"I know. That's what I gave it up for."

It's a good job men are such lousy golfers, or their wives and girlfriends would never see them.

"How is your new student doing?" a golf pro asked an instructor. "Any problems with his game?"
"See for yourself," the instructor replied.
They watched as the student missed shot after shot. Some went only a few yards, while with others he missed the ball completely. In spite of all this, he kept exclaiming, "Great, fantastic, wow, what a shot, what a game!!!!"
"What ever his problem is," the pro commented, "I don't think it's a lack of enthusiasm."

"Did you happen to see a number three ball?" a golfer said to a homeowner.

"Yes I have," the homeowner replied. "In fact, this is it right here, and it broke my window."

"Hmm," the golfer said. "What about a number four ball? Did you happen to see a number four ball?"

A golfer who had been injured by a wayward shot was being loaded into the ambulance.

"I'm afraid I have some bad news for you," a golfing buddy informed him. "I overheard a paramedic say he doesn't think you're going to make it."

As the ambulance drove away with the wailing golfer, his buddy turned to another golfer and said, "I don't see why he's so upset, just because he won't make it to tomorrow's tournament."

"You just can't teach the golfing skills that I possess," a golfer said to his instructor. "I do it all by instinct, you know. These are just natural talents that I happen to bring to the game."

"Oh, thank goodness," the instructor said. "For a while there, I thought that I had taught them to you."

"I threw my dumb golf club into a lake."
"And you're calling your golf club dumb . . . ?"

"This golf course reminds me of my first wife," one golfer said to another. "From a distance they both looked really appealing, but then they got hold of me . . . ."

A golfer decided his game needed some work, so he enrolled in a golf class at the local community center.
"What do you think?" he said to an instructor who had arrived and was watching him practice. "Can you suggest any improvements?"
"Four things," the instructor replied. "First of all, I think your game would be much more effective if you were to take two or three steps before you swing at the ball. Second of all, instead of swinging your arms in an arc, I would suggest bringing your right arm straight back while letting your left arm remain in front of your body. Third of all, I would not bother keeping my eye on the ball during the swing. And fourth of all, I would go over to the football field, because that's where the golf class is. I'm the bowling instructor."

The slice and the hook are what golfers have left after they've forgotten everything else about the game.

"Where is your husband today?" a non golfer's wife asked a golfer's wife.

"He's out playing a round," the golfer's wife replied.

"Oh, you poor dear . . . ."

A golfer, trying to eliminate some bad habits, began to watch other golfers so he could pick up some good habits. He picked up more bad habits.

"Have fun on the golf course," a newlywed wife said as she kissed her husband goodbye.

"Have fun on the pasture," an older wife said to her husband.

"How come I call it a golf course and you call it a pasture?" the newlywed wife said after their husbands had driven away.

"You'll see when they come home," the older wife advised her. "Believe me, the stuff they'll tell us about their games can only be found in a pasture."

Who says that golf isn't good for you. I recently attended the funeral of a man who had been golfing for only a short time, and already he looked ten years younger.

A young boy was showing a friend around his parents home.

"These are my father's golf clubs," he said when they reached the garage. "He says he's going to give them to me and buy a new set for himself as soon as he learns the game."

"How soon do you think that will be?" the friend asked.

"According to my mother," the boy answered, "about another twenty years."

"How come you took up bowling?"

"Because I'm such a terrible golfer."

"Didn't you take lessons from a golf pro?"

"Of course I did. Who do you think suggested bowling?"

"I shot a 78 today," a wife said.

"No kidding," her husband replied.

"Oh, all right. With no kidding, I shot a 97."

"When my husband's golf ball goes into the rough he cusses one way. When it goes into the water he cusses another way. He has a different cuss word for every shot a golfer could ever make, except the one that lands in the fairway."
"What does he say for that one?"
"Holy cow??!!"

"My husband said he would bring me golfing, as long as I didn't embarrass him."
"Where is your husband?"
"He's over there on that family's patio, searching for his golf ball."

"Playing thirty-six holes of golf in one day could affect my physical and emotional well being," one golfer said to another.
"What makes you say that?" the other golfer asked.
"Oh, I didn't say it," the first golfer replied. "My wife did."

"I'd like to talk to you about the great golf game you played today."
"Go ahead, I won't interrupt."

I asked my husband what he would like for his birthday. He said he wanted his golf clubs upgraded. So I had the electrical tape on his grips replaced.

"I'm saving a fortune on golf. I can't afford to get a tee time. I'm telling you, I'm saving a fortune."

"I wonder what it would be like to be married to the greatest golfer in the world," a golfer was asked.
"I don't know," he replied. "You'll have to ask my wife."

All my love to Sheila:

If you should ever wonder why I let Sheila keep score . . . .

When I shoot a seven, she says, "Oh, I don't think you got that much."

"How much do you think I got?" I ask.

"About a five," she says.

"Five it is then," I agree.

That's why I let Sheila keep score.

                                                            Ron

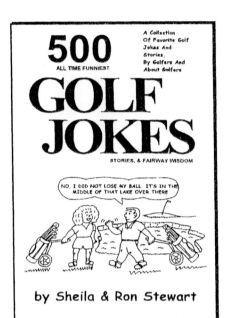

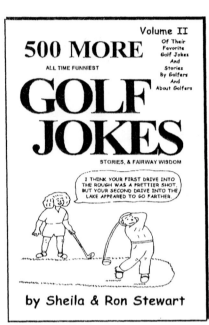

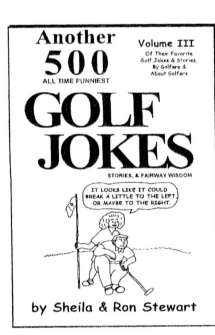

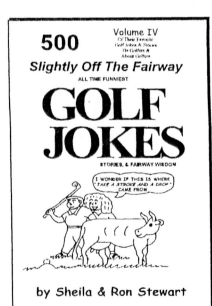

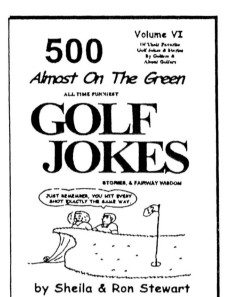

If your local book store does not have a copy of 500 All Time Funniest Golf Jokes, Stories & Fairway Wisdom or our other books, we will be happy to let you know where you can acquire them, or fill your order direct.

Acadia Scale Press

Telephone: 480-496-6191

E-mail: books@acadiascale.com

.

Printed in the United States
1473400003B/241

9 780965 685610